From the kitchen of

TABLE OF CONTENTS

RECIPE TITLE	PAGE

RECIPE TITLE	PAGE

RECIPE TITLE	PAGE

RECIPE TITLE	PAGE

RECIPES

RECIPE TITLE:

CATEGORY:	TOTAL TIME:	PREPARATION: COOKING:

SERVINGS:	RATING:☆☆☆☆☆

INGREDIENTS:

_____

_____

_____

_____

_____

_____

_____

_____

_____

_____

_____

SUBSTITUTIONS/NOTES

_____

_____

_____

DIRECTIONS:

_____

_____

_____

_____

_____

_____

_____

_____

_____

_____

_____

_____

_____

Nutrition Facts
per serving
Calories:
Fat::
Sodium:
Carbs:
Sugars:
Protein:

NOTES:

_____

_____

_____

_____

_____

_____

RECIPE TITLE:

CATEGORY:	TOTAL TIME:	PREPARATION: COOKING:

SERVINGS:	RATING: ☆ ☆ ☆ ☆ ☆

INGREDIENTS:

_____

_____

_____

_____

_____

_____

_____

_____

_____

_____

_____

_____

_____

SUBSTITUTIONS/NOTES

_____

_____

_____

DIRECTIONS:

_____

_____

_____

_____

_____

_____

_____

_____

_____

_____

_____

_____

Nutrition Facts
per serving

Calories:	
Fat::	
Sodium:	
Carbs:	
Sugars:	
Protein:	

NOTES:

_____

_____

_____

_____

_____

_____

RECIPE TITLE:

CATEGORY:	TOTAL TIME:	PREPARATION: COOKING:

SERVINGS:	RATING: ☆☆☆☆☆

INGREDIENTS:

_____

_____

_____

_____

_____

_____

_____

_____

_____

_____

SUBSTITUTIONS/NOTES

_____

_____

_____

DIRECTIONS:

_____

_____

_____

_____

_____

_____

_____

_____

_____

_____

_____

Nutrition Facts per serving
Calories:
Fat::
Sodium:
Carbs:
Sugars:
Protein:

NOTES:

_____

_____

_____

_____

_____

_____

RECIPE TITLE:

CATEGORY:	TOTAL TIME:	*PREPARATION:* *COOKING:*
SERVINGS:	RATING: ☆ ☆ ☆ ☆ ☆	

INGREDIENTS:

_____

_____

_____

_____

_____

_____

_____

_____

_____

_____

_____

_____

SUBSTITUTIONS/NOTES

_____

_____

_____

DIRECTIONS:

_____

_____

_____

_____

_____

_____

_____

_____

_____

_____

_____

Nutrition Facts per serving
Calories:
Fat::
Sodium:
Carbs:
Sugars:
Protein:

NOTES:

_____

_____

_____

_____

_____

RECIPE TITLE:

| CATEGORY: | TOTAL TIME: | *PREPARATION:* |
| | | *COOKING:* |

| SERVINGS: | RATING: ☆☆☆☆☆ |

INGREDIENTS:

_____

_____

_____

_____

_____

_____

_____

_____

_____

_____

_____

_____

SUBSTITUTIONS/NOTES

_____

_____

_____

DIRECTIONS:

_____

_____

_____

_____

_____

_____

_____

_____

_____

_____

_____

_____

_____

Nutrition Facts per serving
Calories:
Fat::
Sodium:
Carbs:
Sugars:
Protein:

NOTES:

_____

_____

_____

_____

_____

RECIPE TITLE:

CATEGORY:	TOTAL TIME:	PREPARATION: COOKING:
SERVINGS:	RATING:☆☆☆☆☆	

INGREDIENTS:

_____

_____

_____

_____

_____

_____

_____

_____

_____

_____

_____

_____

SUBSTITUTIONS/NOTES

_____

_____

_____

DIRECTIONS:

_____

_____

_____

_____

_____

_____

_____

_____

_____

_____

_____

_____

Nutrition Facts
per serving

| Calories: |
| Fat:: |
| Sodium: |
| Carbs: |
| Sugars: |
| Protein: |

NOTES:

_____

_____

_____

_____

_____

RECIPE TITLE:

CATEGORY:	TOTAL TIME:	PREPARATION: COOKING:

SERVINGS: RATING: ☆ ☆ ☆ ☆ ☆

INGREDIENTS:

_____

_____

_____

_____

_____

_____

_____

_____

_____

_____

_____

SUBSTITUTIONS/NOTES

_____

_____

_____

DIRECTIONS:

_____

_____

_____

_____

_____

_____

_____

_____

_____

_____

_____

_____

Nutrition Facts per serving
Calories:
Fat::
Sodium:
Carbs:
Sugars:
Protein:

NOTES:

_____

_____

_____

_____

_____

_____

RECIPE TITLE:

CATEGORY:	TOTAL TIME:	PREPARATION: COOKING:

SERVINGS: RATING: ☆ ☆ ☆ ☆ ☆

INGREDIENTS:

_____

_____

_____

_____

_____

_____

_____

_____

_____

_____

_____

_____

SUBSTITUTIONS/NOTES

_____

_____

_____

DIRECTIONS:

_____

_____

_____

_____

_____

_____

_____

_____

_____

_____

_____

| **Nutrition Facts** |
| per serving |
| Calories: |
| Fat:: |
| Sodium: |
| Carbs: |
| Sugars: |
| Protein: |

NOTES:

_____

_____

_____

_____

_____

_____

RECIPE TITLE:

CATEGORY:	TOTAL TIME:	PREPARATION: COOKING:
SERVINGS:	RATING: ☆☆☆☆☆	

INGREDIENTS:

_____

_____

_____

_____

_____

_____

_____

_____

_____

_____

_____

_____

_____

SUBSTITUTIONS/NOTES

_____

_____

_____

DIRECTIONS:

_____

_____

_____

_____

_____

_____

_____

_____

_____

_____

_____

_____

Nutrition Facts
per serving
Calories:
Fat::
Sodium:
Carbs:
Sugars:
Protein:

NOTES:

_____

_____

_____

_____

_____

_____

RECIPE TITLE:

CATEGORY:	TOTAL TIME:	PREPARATION: COOKING:

SERVINGS:	RATING: ☆☆☆☆☆

INGREDIENTS:

_____

_____

_____

_____

_____

_____

_____

_____

_____

_____

_____

_____

SUBSTITUTIONS/NOTES

_____

_____

_____

DIRECTIONS:

Nutrition Facts per serving
Calories:
Fat::
Sodium:
Carbs:
Sugars:
Protein:

NOTES:

RECEIPE TITLE:

CATEGORY:	TOTAL TIME:	PREPARATION: COOKING:

SERVINGS:	RATING: ☆☆☆☆☆

INGREDIENTS:

_____

_____

_____

_____

_____

_____

_____

_____

_____

_____

_____

_____

SUBSTITUTIONS/NOTES

_____

_____

_____

DIRECTIONS:

_____

_____

_____

_____

_____

_____

_____

_____

_____

_____

_____

Nutrition Facts per serving
Calories:
Fat::
Sodium:
Carbs:
Sugars:
Protein:

NOTES:

_____

_____

_____

_____

_____

RECIPE TITLE:

CATEGORY:	TOTAL TIME:	PREPARATION: COOKING:

SERVINGS:	RATING: ☆ ☆ ☆ ☆ ☆

INGREDIENTS:

_____

_____

_____

_____

_____

_____

_____

_____

_____

_____

_____

SUBSTITUTIONS/NOTES

_____

_____

_____

DIRECTIONS:

_____

_____

_____

_____

_____

_____

_____

_____

_____

_____

_____

_____

Nutrition Facts per serving
Calories:
Fat::
Sodium:
Carbs:
Sugars:
Protein:

NOTES:

_____

_____

_____

_____

_____

_____

RECIPE TITLE:

CATEGORY:	TOTAL TIME:	PREPARATION: COOKING:

SERVINGS:	RATING: ☆ ☆ ☆ ☆ ☆

INGREDIENTS:

_____

_____

_____

_____

_____

_____

_____

_____

_____

_____

_____

_____

_____

SUBSTITUTIONS/NOTES

_____

_____

_____

DIRECTIONS:

_____

_____

_____

_____

_____

_____

_____

_____

_____

_____

_____

Nutrition Facts per serving	**NOTES:**
Calories:	_____
Fat::	_____
Sodium:	_____
Carbs:	_____
Sugars:	_____
Protein:	_____

RECIPE TITLE:

| CATEGORY: | TOTAL TIME: | PREPARATION: |
| | | COOKING: |

| SERVINGS: | RATING:☆☆☆☆☆ |

INGREDIENTS:

_____

_____

_____

_____

_____

_____

_____

_____

_____

_____

_____

_____

SUBSTITUTIONS/NOTES

_____

_____

_____

DIRECTIONS:

_____

_____

_____

_____

_____

_____

_____

_____

_____

_____

_____

_____

Nutrition Facts per serving
Calories:
Fat::
Sodium:
Carbs:
Sugars:
Protein:

NOTES:

_____

_____

_____

_____

_____

_____

RECIPE TITLE:

CATEGORY:	TOTAL TIME:	PREPARATION: COOKING:

SERVINGS: RATING: ☆ ☆ ☆ ☆ ☆

INGREDIENTS:

_____

_____

_____

_____

_____

_____

_____

_____

_____

_____

_____

_____

SUBSTITUTIONS/NOTES

_____

_____

_____

DIRECTIONS:

_____

_____

_____

_____

_____

_____

_____

_____

_____

_____

_____

_____

_____

Nutrition Facts per serving
Calories:
Fat::
Sodium:
Carbs:
Sugars:
Protein:

NOTES:

_____

_____

_____

_____

_____

_____

RECIPE TITLE:

| CATEGORY: | TOTAL TIME: | PREPARATION: |
| | | COOKING: |

SERVINGS: RATING: ☆ ☆ ☆ ☆ ☆

INGREDIENTS:

_____

_____

_____

_____

_____

_____

_____

_____

_____

_____

_____

_____

SUBSTITUTIONS/NOTES

_____

_____

_____

DIRECTIONS:

_____

_____

_____

_____

_____

_____

_____

_____

_____

_____

_____

_____

Nutrition Facts per serving
Calories:
Fat::
Sodium:
Carbs:
Sugars:
Protein:

NOTES:

_____

_____

_____

_____

_____

RECIPE TITLE:

CATEGORY:	TOTAL TIME:	PREPARATION: COOKING:
SERVINGS:	RATING:☆☆☆☆☆	

INGREDIENTS:

_____

_____

_____

_____

_____

_____

_____

_____

_____

_____

_____

_____

SUBSTITUTIONS/NOTES

_____

_____

_____

DIRECTIONS:

_____

_____

_____

_____

_____

_____

_____

_____

_____

_____

_____

Nutrition Facts per serving
Calories:
Fat::
Sodium:
Carbs:
Sugars:
Protein:

NOTES:

_____

_____

_____

_____

_____

_____

RECIPE TITLE:

CATEGORY:	TOTAL TIME:	PREPARATION: COOKING:

SERVINGS:	RATING: ☆ ☆ ☆ ☆ ☆

INGREDIENTS:

_____

_____

_____

_____

_____

_____

_____

_____

_____

_____

_____

_____

SUBSTITUTIONS/NOTES

_____

_____

_____

DIRECTIONS:

_____

_____

_____

_____

_____

_____

_____

_____

_____

_____

_____

Nutrition Facts
per serving

Calories:	
Fat::	
Sodium:	
Carbs:	
Sugars:	
Protein:	

NOTES:

_____

_____

_____

_____

_____

_____

RECIPE TITLE:

| CATEGORY: | TOTAL TIME: | PREPARATION: |
| | | COOKING: |

| SERVINGS: | RATING: ☆☆☆☆☆ |

INGREDIENTS:

_____

_____

_____

_____

_____

_____

_____

_____

_____

_____

_____

SUBSTITUTIONS/NOTES

_____

_____

_____

DIRECTIONS:

_____

_____

_____

_____

_____

_____

_____

_____

_____

_____

_____

_____

Nutrition Facts
per serving

| Calories: |
| Fat:: |
| Sodium: |
| Carbs: |
| Sugars: |
| Protein: |

NOTES:

_____

_____

_____

_____

_____

_____

RECIPE TITLE:

| CATEGORY: | TOTAL TIME: | PREPARATION: |
| | | COOKING: |

| SERVINGS: | RATING: ☆☆☆☆☆ |

INGREDIENTS:

_____

_____

_____

_____

_____

_____

_____

_____

_____

_____

_____

_____

SUBSTITUTIONS/NOTES

_____

_____

_____

DIRECTIONS:

_____

_____

_____

_____

_____

_____

_____

_____

_____

_____

_____

_____

_____

Nutrition Facts per serving
Calories:
Fat::
Sodium:
Carbs:
Sugars:
Protein:

NOTES:

_____

_____

_____

_____

_____

RECIPE TITLE:

CATEGORY:	TOTAL TIME:	PREPARATION: COOKING:
SERVINGS:	RATING: ☆☆☆☆☆	

INGREDIENTS:

SUBSTITUTIONS/NOTES

DIRECTIONS:

_____

_____

_____

_____

_____

_____

_____

_____

_____

_____

_____

Nutrition Facts per serving
Calories:
Fat::
Sodium:
Carbs:
Sugars:
Protein:

NOTES:

_____

_____

_____

_____

_____

_____

RECIPE TITLE:

CATEGORY:	TOTAL TIME:	*PREPARATION:* *COOKING:*
SERVINGS:	RATING: ☆☆☆☆☆	

INGREDIENTS:

_____

_____

_____

_____

_____

_____

_____

_____

_____

_____

_____

SUBSTITUTIONS/NOTES

_____

_____

_____

DIRECTIONS:

_____

_____

_____

_____

_____

_____

_____

_____

_____

_____

_____

Nutrition Facts per serving
Calories:
Fat::
Sodium:
Carbs:
Sugars:
Protein:

NOTES:

_____

_____

_____

_____

_____

_____

RECIPE TITLE:

| CATEGORY: | TOTAL TIME: | PREPARATION: |
| | | COOKING: |

| SERVINGS: | RATING: ☆☆☆☆☆ |

INGREDIENTS:

_____

_____

_____

_____

_____

_____

_____

_____

_____

_____

_____

SUBSTITUTIONS/NOTES

_____

_____

_____

DIRECTIONS:

_____

_____

_____

_____

_____

_____

_____

_____

_____

_____

_____

Nutrition Facts
per serving

Calories:

Fat::

Sodium:

Carbs:

Sugars:

Protein:

NOTES:

_____

_____

_____

_____

_____

_____

RECIPE TITLE:

| CATEGORY: | TOTAL TIME: | PREPARATION: |
| | | COOKING: |

| SERVINGS: | RATING: ☆☆☆☆☆ |

INGREDIENTS:

_____

_____

_____

_____

_____

_____

_____

_____

_____

_____

_____

_____

SUBSTITUTIONS/NOTES

_____

_____

_____

DIRECTIONS:

_____

_____

_____

_____

_____

_____

_____

_____

_____

_____

_____

Nutrition Facts per serving	NOTES:
Calories:	
Fat::	
Sodium:	
Carbs:	
Sugars:	
Protein:	

RECIPE TITLE:

| CATEGORY: | TOTAL TIME: | *PREPARATION:* |
| | | *COOKING:* |

| SERVINGS: | RATING: ☆ ☆ ☆ ☆ ☆ |

INGREDIENTS:

_____

_____

_____

_____

_____

_____

_____

_____

_____

_____

_____

_____

SUBSTITUTIONS/NOTES

_____

_____

_____

DIRECTIONS:

_____

_____

_____

_____

_____

_____

_____

_____

_____

_____

_____

Nutrition Facts
per serving

Calories:	
Fat::	
Sodium:	
Carbs:	
Sugars:	
Protein:	

NOTES:

_____

_____

_____

_____

_____

_____

RECIPE TITLE:

CATEGORY:	TOTAL TIME:	PREPARATION: COOKING:
SERVINGS:	RATING:☆☆☆☆☆	

INGREDIENTS:

_____

_____

_____

_____

_____

_____

_____

_____

_____

_____

_____

SUBSTITUTIONS/NOTES

_____

_____

_____

DIRECTIONS:

_____

_____

_____

_____

_____

_____

_____

_____

_____

_____

_____

_____

_____

Nutrition Facts per serving
Calories:
Fat::
Sodium:
Carbs:
Sugars:
Protein:

NOTES:

_____

_____

_____

_____

_____

_____

RECIPE TITLE:

CATEGORY:	TOTAL TIME:	PREPARATION: COOKING:

SERVINGS:	RATING: ☆ ☆ ☆ ☆ ☆

INGREDIENTS:

_____

_____

_____

_____

_____

_____

_____

_____

_____

_____

_____

SUBSTITUTIONS/NOTES

_____

_____

_____

DIRECTIONS:

_____

_____

_____

_____

_____

_____

_____

_____

_____

_____

_____

_____

Nutrition Facts per serving
Calories:
Fat::
Sodium:
Carbs:
Sugars:
Protein:

NOTES:

_____

_____

_____

_____

_____

_____

RECIPE TITLE:

CATEGORY:	TOTAL TIME:	PREPARATION: COOKING:
SERVINGS:	RATING: ☆☆☆☆☆	

INGREDIENTS:

_____

_____

_____

_____

_____

_____

_____

_____

_____

_____

_____

_____

SUBSTITUTIONS/NOTES

_____

_____

_____

DIRECTIONS:

_____

_____

_____

_____

_____

_____

_____

_____

_____

_____

_____

_____

| **Nutrition Facts** |
| per serving |
| Calories: |
| Fat:: |
| Sodium: |
| Carbs: |
| Sugars: |
| Protein: |

NOTES:

_____

_____

_____

_____

_____

RECIPE TITLE:

CATEGORY:	TOTAL TIME:	PREPARATION: COOKING:
SERVINGS:	RATING:☆☆☆☆☆	

INGREDIENTS:

_____

_____

_____

_____

_____

_____

_____

_____

_____

_____

_____

_____

SUBSTITUTIONS/NOTES

_____

_____

_____

DIRECTIONS:

_____

_____

_____

_____

_____

_____

_____

_____

_____

_____

_____

Nutrition Facts
per serving
Calories:
Fat::
Sodium:
Carbs:
Sugars:
Protein:

NOTES:

_____

_____

_____

_____

_____

_____

RECIPE TITLE:

| CATEGORY: | TOTAL TIME: | PREPARATION: |
| | | COOKING: |

SERVINGS: RATING: ☆☆☆☆☆

INGREDIENTS:

_____

_____

_____

_____

_____

_____

_____

_____

_____

_____

_____

SUBSTITUTIONS/NOTES

_____

_____

_____

DIRECTIONS:

_____

_____

_____

_____

_____

_____

_____

_____

_____

_____

_____

_____

| **Nutrition Facts** |
| per serving |
| Calories: |
| Fat:: |
| Sodium: |
| Carbs: |
| Sugars: |
| Protein: |

NOTES:

_____

_____

_____

_____

_____

_____

RECIPE TITLE:

CATEGORY:	TOTAL TIME:	PREPARATION: COOKING:

SERVINGS: RATING: ☆☆☆☆☆

INGREDIENTS:

_____

_____

_____

_____

_____

_____

_____

_____

_____

_____

_____

_____

SUBSTITUTIONS/NOTES

_____

_____

_____

DIRECTIONS:

_____

_____

_____

_____

_____

_____

_____

_____

_____

_____

_____

Nutrition Facts
per serving

Calories:	
Fat::	
Sodium:	
Carbs:	
Sugars:	
Protein:	

NOTES:

_____

_____

_____

_____

_____

_____

RECIPE TITLE:

CATEGORY:	TOTAL TIME:	PREPARATION: COOKING:

SERVINGS:	RATING: ☆☆☆☆☆

INGREDIENTS:

_____

_____

_____

_____

_____

_____

_____

_____

_____

_____

_____

_____

SUBSTITUTIONS/NOTES

_____

_____

_____

DIRECTIONS:

_____

_____

_____

_____

_____

_____

_____

_____

_____

_____

_____

_____

Nutrition Facts per serving
Calories:
Fat::
Sodium:
Carbs:
Sugars:
Protein:

NOTES:

_____

_____

_____

_____

_____

_____

RECIPE TITLE:

CATEGORY:	TOTAL TIME:	PREPARATION: COOKING:

SERVINGS:	RATING: ☆ ☆ ☆ ☆ ☆

INGREDIENTS:

_____

_____

_____

_____

_____

_____

_____

_____

_____

_____

_____

_____

SUBSTITUTIONS/NOTES

_____

_____

_____

DIRECTIONS:

_____

_____

_____

_____

_____

_____

_____

_____

_____

_____

_____

| **Nutrition Facts** |
| per serving |
| Calories: |
| Fat:: |
| Sodium: |
| Carbs: |
| Sugars: |
| Protein: |

NOTES:

_____

_____

_____

_____

_____

_____

RECIPE TITLE:

| CATEGORY: | TOTAL TIME: | PREPARATION: |
| | | COOKING: |

| SERVINGS: | RATING: ☆☆☆☆☆ |

INGREDIENTS:

_____

_____

_____

_____

_____

_____

_____

_____

_____

_____

_____

_____

_____

SUBSTITUTIONS/NOTES

_____

_____

_____

DIRECTIONS:

_____

_____

_____

_____

_____

_____

_____

_____

_____

_____

_____

_____

Nutrition Facts per serving
Calories:
Fat::
Sodium:
Carbs:
Sugars:
Protein:

NOTES:

_____

_____

_____

_____

_____

_____

RECIPE TITLE:

| CATEGORY: | TOTAL TIME: | PREPARATION: |
| | | COOKING: |

| SERVINGS: | RATING: ☆ ☆ ☆ ☆ ☆ |

INGREDIENTS:

_____

_____

_____

_____

_____

_____

_____

_____

_____

_____

_____

_____

SUBSTITUTIONS/NOTES

_____

_____

_____

DIRECTIONS:

_____

_____

_____

_____

_____

_____

_____

_____

_____

_____

_____

Nutrition Facts per serving
Calories:
Fat::
Sodium:
Carbs:
Sugars:
Protein:

NOTES:

_____

_____

_____

_____

_____

_____

RECIPE TITLE:

CATEGORY:	TOTAL TIME:	PREPARATION: COOKING:

SERVINGS:	RATING: ☆☆☆☆☆

INGREDIENTS:

_____

_____

_____

_____

_____

_____

_____

_____

_____

_____

_____

_____

SUBSTITUTIONS/NOTES

_____

_____

_____

DIRECTIONS:

_____

_____

_____

_____

_____

_____

_____

_____

_____

_____

_____

Nutrition Facts
per serving

Calories:	
Fat::	
Sodium:	
Carbs:	
Sugars:	
Protein:	

NOTES:

_____

_____

_____

_____

_____

_____

RECIPE TITLE:

CATEGORY:	TOTAL TIME:	PREPARATION: COOKING:

SERVINGS:	RATING:☆☆☆☆☆

INGREDIENTS:

_____

_____

_____

_____

_____

_____

_____

_____

_____

_____

_____

_____

_____

SUBSTITUTIONS/NOTES

_____

_____

_____

DIRECTIONS:

_____

_____

_____

_____

_____

_____

_____

_____

_____

_____

_____

Nutrition Facts per serving
Calories:
Fat::
Sodium:
Carbs:
Sugars:
Protein:

NOTES:

_____

_____

_____

_____

_____

_____

RECIPE TITLE:

CATEGORY:	TOTAL TIME:	PREPARATION: COOKING:

SERVINGS:	RATING: ☆☆☆☆☆

INGREDIENTS:

_____

_____

_____

_____

_____

_____

_____

_____

_____

_____

_____

_____

SUBSTITUTIONS/NOTES

_____

_____

_____

DIRECTIONS:

_____

_____

_____

_____

_____

_____

_____

_____

_____

_____

_____

_____

Nutrition Facts per serving
Calories:
Fat::
Sodium:
Carbs:
Sugars:
Protein:

NOTES:

_____

_____

_____

_____

_____

_____

RECIPE TITLE:

CATEGORY:	TOTAL TIME:	PREPARATION: COOKING:

SERVINGS:	RATING: ☆ ☆ ☆ ☆ ☆

INGREDIENTS:

_____

_____

_____

_____

_____

_____

_____

_____

_____

_____

_____

_____

SUBSTITUTIONS/NOTES

_____

_____

_____

DIRECTIONS:

_____

_____

_____

_____

_____

_____

_____

_____

_____

_____

_____

Nutrition Facts
per serving

Calories:
Fat::
Sodium:
Carbs:
Sugars:
Protein:

NOTES:

_____

_____

_____

_____

_____

_____

RECIPE TITLE:

CATEGORY:	TOTAL TIME:	PREPARATION: COOKING:
SERVINGS:	RATING:☆☆☆☆☆	

INGREDIENTS:

_____

_____

_____

_____

_____

_____

_____

_____

_____

_____

_____

SUBSTITUTIONS/NOTES

_____

_____

_____

DIRECTIONS:

_____

_____

_____

_____

_____

_____

_____

_____

_____

_____

_____

_____

Nutrition Facts per serving
Calories:
Fat::
Sodium:
Carbs:
Sugars:
Protein:

NOTES:

_____

_____

_____

_____

_____

_____

RECIPE TITLE:

CATEGORY:	TOTAL TIME:	PREPARATION: COOKING:
SERVINGS:		RATING: ☆☆☆☆☆

INGREDIENTS:

_____

_____

_____

_____

_____

_____

_____

_____

_____

_____

_____

SUBSTITUTIONS/NOTES

_____

_____

_____

DIRECTIONS:

_____

_____

_____

_____

_____

_____

_____

_____

_____

_____

_____

_____

| **Nutrition Facts** |
| per serving |
| Calories: |
| Fat:: |
| Sodium: |
| Carbs: |
| Sugars: |
| Protein: |

NOTES:

_____

_____

_____

_____

_____

_____

RECIPE TITLE:

CATEGORY:	TOTAL TIME:	PREPARATION:
		COOKING:

SERVINGS:	RATING: ☆☆☆☆☆

INGREDIENTS:

_____

_____

_____

_____

_____

_____

_____

_____

_____

_____

_____

_____

SUBSTITUTIONS/NOTES

_____

_____

_____

DIRECTIONS:

_____

_____

_____

_____

_____

_____

_____

_____

_____

_____

_____

Nutrition Facts per serving
Calories:
Fat::
Sodium:
Carbs:
Sugars:
Protein:

NOTES:

_____

_____

_____

_____

_____

_____

RECIPE TITLE:

CATEGORY:	TOTAL TIME:	PREPARATION: COOKING:

SERVINGS:	RATING: ☆☆☆☆☆

INGREDIENTS:

_____

_____

_____

_____

_____

_____

_____

_____

_____

_____

_____

_____

SUBSTITUTIONS/NOTES

_____

_____

_____

DIRECTIONS:

_____

_____

_____

_____

_____

_____

_____

_____

_____

_____

_____

Nutrition Facts per serving
Calories:
Fat::
Sodium:
Carbs:
Sugars:
Protein:

NOTES:

_____

_____

_____

_____

_____

_____

RECIPE TITLE:

CATEGORY:	TOTAL TIME:	PREPARATION: COOKING:

SERVINGS:	RATING: ☆ ☆ ☆ ☆ ☆

INGREDIENTS:

_____

_____

_____

_____

_____

_____

_____

_____

_____

_____

_____

_____

SUBSTITUTIONS/NOTES

_____

_____

_____

DIRECTIONS:

_____

_____

_____

_____

_____

_____

_____

_____

_____

_____

_____

_____

Nutrition Facts
per serving

Calories:

Fat::

Sodium:

Carbs:

  Sugars:

Protein:

NOTES:

_____

_____

_____

_____

_____

_____

RECIPE TITLE:

CATEGORY:	TOTAL TIME:	PREPARATION: COOKING:
SERVINGS:		RATING: ☆☆☆☆☆

INGREDIENTS:

_____

_____

_____

_____

_____

_____

_____

_____

_____

_____

_____

SUBSTITUTIONS/NOTES

_____

_____

_____

DIRECTIONS:

_____

_____

_____

_____

_____

_____

_____

_____

_____

_____

_____

Nutrition Facts per serving
Calories:
Fat::
Sodium:
Carbs:
Sugars:
Protein:

NOTES:

_____

_____

_____

_____

_____

_____

RECIPE TITLE:

| CATEGORY: | TOTAL TIME: | PREPARATION: |
| | | COOKING: |

| SERVINGS: | RATING: ☆☆☆☆☆ |

INGREDIENTS:

_____

_____

_____

_____

_____

_____

_____

_____

_____

_____

_____

_____

_____

SUBSTITUTIONS/NOTES

_____

_____

_____

DIRECTIONS:

_____

_____

_____

_____

_____

_____

_____

_____

_____

_____

Nutrition Facts per serving
Calories:
Fat::
Sodium:
Carbs:
Sugars:
Protein:

NOTES:

_____

_____

_____

_____

_____

RECIPE TITLE:

CATEGORY:	TOTAL TIME:	PREPARATION: COOKING:

SERVINGS: RATING: ☆ ☆ ☆ ☆ ☆

INGREDIENTS:

_____

_____

_____

_____

_____

_____

_____

_____

_____

_____

_____

_____

_____

SUBSTITUTIONS/NOTES

_____

_____

_____

DIRECTIONS:

_____

_____

_____

_____

_____

_____

_____

_____

_____

_____

_____

Nutrition Facts per serving
Calories:
Fat::
Sodium:
Carbs:
Sugars:
Protein:

NOTES:

_____

_____

_____

_____

_____

_____

RECIPE TITLE:

| CATEGORY: | TOTAL TIME: | PREPARATION: |
| | | COOKING: |

| SERVINGS: | RATING: ☆☆☆☆☆ |

INGREDIENTS:

_____

_____

_____

_____

_____

_____

_____

_____

_____

_____

_____

_____

SUBSTITUTIONS/NOTES

_____

_____

_____

DIRECTIONS:

_____

_____

_____

_____

_____

_____

_____

_____

_____

_____

_____

_____

Nutrition Facts per serving	**NOTES:**
Calories:	
Fat::	
Sodium:	
Carbs:	
Sugars:	
Protein:	

RECIPE TITLE:

| CATEGORY: | TOTAL TIME: | PREPARATION: |
| | | COOKING: |

| SERVINGS: | RATING: ☆☆☆☆☆ |

INGREDIENTS:

_____

_____

_____

_____

_____

_____

_____

_____

_____

_____

_____

SUBSTITUTIONS/NOTES

_____

_____

_____

DIRECTIONS:

_____

_____

_____

_____

_____

_____

_____

_____

_____

_____

_____

Nutrition Facts per serving
Calories:
Fat::
Sodium:
Carbs:
Sugars:
Protein:

NOTES:

_____

_____

_____

_____

_____

RECIPE TITLE:

CATEGORY:	TOTAL TIME:	PREPARATION: COOKING:

SERVINGS:	RATING: ☆☆☆☆☆

INGREDIENTS:

_____

_____

_____

_____

_____

_____

_____

_____

_____

_____

_____

_____

SUBSTITUTIONS/NOTES

_____

_____

_____

DIRECTIONS:

_____

_____

_____

_____

_____

_____

_____

_____

_____

_____

_____

_____

Nutrition Facts per serving
Calories:
Fat::
Sodium:
Carbs:
Sugars:
Protein:

NOTES:

_____

_____

_____

_____

_____

_____

RECIPE TITLE:

CATEGORY:	TOTAL TIME:	PREPARATION: COOKING:

SERVINGS:	RATING: ☆☆☆☆☆

INGREDIENTS:

_____

_____

_____

_____

_____

_____

_____

_____

_____

_____

_____

SUBSTITUTIONS/NOTES

_____

_____

_____

DIRECTIONS:

_____

_____

_____

_____

_____

_____

_____

_____

_____

_____

_____

Nutrition Facts per serving
Calories:
Fat::
Sodium:
Carbs:
Sugars:
Protein:

NOTES:

_____

_____

_____

_____

_____

_____

RECIPE TITLE:

CATEGORY:	TOTAL TIME:	PREPARATION: COOKING:

SERVINGS: RATING: ☆ ☆ ☆ ☆ ☆

INGREDIENTS:

_____

_____

_____

_____

_____

_____

_____

_____

_____

_____

_____

_____

SUBSTITUTIONS/NOTES

_____

_____

_____

DIRECTIONS:

_____

_____

_____

_____

_____

_____

_____

_____

_____

_____

_____

Nutrition Facts per serving
Calories:
Fat::
Sodium:
Carbs:
Sugars:
Protein:

NOTES:

_____

_____

_____

_____

_____

_____

RECIPE TITLE:

CATEGORY: TOTAL TIME: *PREPARATION:*
                                            COOKING:

SERVINGS: RATING: ☆ ☆ ☆ ☆ ☆

INGREDIENTS:

_____

_____

_____

_____

_____

_____

_____

_____

_____

_____

_____

_____

SUBSTITUTIONS/NOTES

_____

_____

_____

DIRECTIONS:

_____

_____

_____

_____

_____

_____

_____

_____

_____

_____

_____

Nutrition Facts per serving
Calories:
Fat::
Sodium:
Carbs:
Sugars:
Protein:

NOTES:

_____

_____

_____

_____

_____

_____

RECIPE TITLE:

CATEGORY:　　　　TOTAL TIME:　　　PREPARATION:
　　　　　　　　　　　　　　　　　　COOKING:

SERVINGS:　　　　　　　RATING: ☆ ☆ ☆ ☆ ☆

INGREDIENTS:

_____

_____

_____

_____

_____

_____

_____

_____

_____

_____

_____

_____

_____

SUBSTITUTIONS/NOTES

_____

_____

_____

DIRECTIONS:

_____

_____

_____

_____

_____

_____

_____

_____

_____

_____

Nutrition Facts per serving
Calories:
Fat::
Sodium:
Carbs:
Sugars:
Protein:

NOTES:

_____

_____

_____

_____

_____

_____

RECIPE TITLE:

CATEGORY:	TOTAL TIME:	PREPARATION: COOKING:

SERVINGS:	RATING: ☆☆☆☆☆

INGREDIENTS:

_____

_____

_____

_____

_____

_____

_____

_____

_____

_____

_____

_____

SUBSTITUTIONS/NOTES

_____

_____

_____

DIRECTIONS:

_____

_____

_____

_____

_____

_____

_____

_____

_____

_____

_____

Nutrition Facts
per serving

Calories:
Fat::
Sodium:
Carbs:
Sugars:
Protein:

NOTES:

_____

_____

_____

_____

_____

_____

RECIPE TITLE:

CATEGORY:	TOTAL TIME:	PREPARATION: COOKING:

SERVINGS:	RATING:☆☆☆☆☆

INGREDIENTS:

_____

_____

_____

_____

_____

_____

_____

_____

_____

_____

_____

_____

_____

SUBSTITUTIONS/NOTES

_____

_____

_____

DIRECTIONS:

_____

_____

_____

_____

_____

_____

_____

_____

_____

_____

_____

_____

Nutrition Facts per serving
Calories:
Fat::
Sodium:
Carbs:
Sugars:
Protein:

NOTES:

_____

_____

_____

_____

_____

_____

RECIPE TITLE:

| CATEGORY: | TOTAL TIME: | PREPARATION: |
| | | COOKING: |

| SERVINGS: | RATING: ☆☆☆☆☆ |

INGREDIENTS:

_____

_____

_____

_____

_____

_____

_____

_____

_____

_____

_____

SUBSTITUTIONS/NOTES

_____

_____

_____

DIRECTIONS:

_____

_____

_____

_____

_____

_____

_____

_____

_____

_____

Nutrition Facts per serving
Calories:
Fat::
Sodium:
Carbs:
Sugars:
Protein:

NOTES:

_____

_____

_____

_____

_____

RECIPE TITLE:

CATEGORY:	TOTAL TIME:	PREPARATION: COOKING:

SERVINGS:	RATING: ☆☆☆☆☆

INGREDIENTS:

_____

_____

_____

_____

_____

_____

_____

_____

_____

_____

_____

_____

SUBSTITUTIONS/NOTES

_____

_____

_____

DIRECTIONS:

_____

_____

_____

_____

_____

_____

_____

_____

_____

_____

Nutrition Facts per serving
Calories:
Fat::
Sodium:
Carbs:
Sugars:
Protein:

NOTES:

_____

_____

_____

_____

_____

_____

RECIPE TITLE:

CATEGORY: TOTAL TIME: *PREPARATION:*
                                  COOKING:

SERVINGS: RATING: ☆ ☆ ☆ ☆ ☆

INGREDIENTS:

_____

_____

_____

_____

_____

_____

_____

_____

_____

_____

_____

_____

_____

SUBSTITUTIONS/NOTES

_____

_____

_____

DIRECTIONS:

_____

_____

_____

_____

_____

_____

_____

_____

_____

_____

_____

Nutrition Facts per serving	
Calories:	
Fat::	
Sodium:	
Carbs:	
Sugars:	
Protein:	

NOTES:

_____

_____

_____

_____

_____

RECIPE TITLE:

CATEGORY:	TOTAL TIME:	PREPARATION: COOKING:
SERVINGS:	RATING: ☆☆☆☆☆	

INGREDIENTS:

_____

_____

_____

_____

_____

_____

_____

_____

_____

_____

_____

SUBSTITUTIONS/NOTES

_____

_____

_____

DIRECTIONS:

_____

_____

_____

_____

_____

_____

_____

_____

_____

_____

_____

Nutrition Facts
per serving

| Calories: |
| Fat:: |
| Sodium: |
| Carbs: |
| Sugars: |
| Protein: |

NOTES:

_____

_____

_____

_____

_____

_____

Notes	Page

Notes | Page

COMMON KITCHEN CONVERSIONS

MEASURE	FLUID OZ	TBSP	TSP
4 cup	1 quart	64 tbsp	192 tsp
2 cup	1 pint	32 tbsp	96 tsp
1 cup	8 oz	16 tbsp	48 tsp
3/4 cup	6 oz	12 tbsp	36 tsp
2/3 cup	5 oz	11 tbsp	32 tsp
1/2 cup	4 oz	8 tbsp	24 tsp
1/3 cup	3 oz	5 tbsp	16 tsp
¼ cup	2 oz	4 tbsp	12 tsp
1/8 cup	1 oz	2 tbsp	6 tsp
1/16 cup	.5 oz	1 tbsp	3 tsp